# *Christmas & W* *Volume*

CH00519605

## Black Bough Poetry

Editor: Matthew M. C. Smith

Sub-editors: Damien B. Donnelly, M.S. Evans

Artist: Emma Bissonnet

www.blackboughpoetry.com
Twitter: @blackboughpoems
FB: BlackBoughpoetry
Insta: Black Bough Poetry

First published in print by Black Bough Poetry in 2021.

*Editorial note:*

Welcome to our second Christmas and winter edition, volume 2. Once again, it's a privilege to curate a festive collection of stunning poems alongside Emma Bissonnet's artwork. In this book, we feature the work of over sixty writers and include some short poetic prose. This is a volume to dip in and out of - rich, condensed, imagistic work about Christmas and other winter festivals. The poets take us to frozen, bleak landscapes within and without and through the blasts of arctic winds, through dark snowstorms to memory-orbs of warmth and illumination.

This has been a bittersweet year for so many of us. The global pandemic persists; immense suffering is endured in war-torn states. The news is dominated by stories of hardship and environmental crises. In this small volume of poetry, we are reminded what it is to be human—the joy of connection, the nostalgia of memories, the pain of loss. A very human collection where snow brings silence, purity, innocent pleasure and pathos.

After the publication of Dai Fry's chapbook *Under Photon Crowns*, followed by the sad news of his passing, the publication of *Dark Confessions* and *Freedom-rapture* to commemorate 50 years since Jim Morrison's passing and running 51 weeks of #TopTweetTuesday there'll be a break on publications for *Black Bough Poetry*. But we'll be publishing the follow-up to this festive edition next year, continuing with the 'Silver Branch' project and one or two surprises.

Many thanks to the *Black Bough* team for this collection — Damien B. Donnelly and M.S. Evans who've not only provided great work but cast a critical eye over the volume. And, of course, Emma Bissonnet, an immensely talented professional artist based in Swansea. Thanks for the outstanding support this year.

We hope you enjoy this work and come back for more in 2022.

Best wishes,

*Matthew M. C. Smith*
Editor—Black Bough Poetry

Illustrations by Emma Bissonnet. For details go to page 49.

Cover image: Maple Fox
                Little Owl p. 1.
                Swallows p. 27.
                Winter Solstice, Mari Lwyd p. 40.
                Swallows of the Valley, Pennard Castle, Gower p. 51.

# Contents

## Beacons

Figures bright on the ice-white moor,
slope-bound to the wilderness;
ink of voices dyeing the snow.

A clatter of sledges, riot of children
and barking. Small fingers point
to the winding wing, conducting its
shadow. It vanishes

over verglas peak, its cry
as cold as frost-stone.

*Matthew M. C. Smith*


## Winter Flow

On bleak days, the river's braided waves roil
in winter's leaden waters, reflecting nothing
as sullen sky glares down at broken
dreams of leaves, ducks huddled on icy banks
all colours muted – earth sucks back life
into winter's graveyard.
I retreat into my own yard, barren now
to await the world's resurgence.

*Adrienne Stevenson*

## A Snow Day

Today the track is impassable,
a windfall of time blesses my hands.

I watch my small world unfold
in newspaper tones of ink and snow.

In the field rooks squabble
over bruised stubbles of barley,

a surprise of hares nibble at frost,
searching for the green spectre of spring.

*Lynn Valentine*


## Filoplume

Blue night has seized this moss-spread plot.
From the petrified rosehip branch
to the kiss-chasing grosbeak,
her pale breast puffed, filoplumes a quiver.

The moon, in mollifying mood
pats her charge, oversees the expectant pulse

and as diurnal rhythm slows, she watches
each leaf and bramble, each tiny fragment
consumed by the full barn-mouth agape,
chewing on sea-scented hush.

*Lucy Holme*

## Kindling

Already the light is leaving.
See the afternoon pack its bags with a steady shrug,
smelling of a season still a month away.

We are gathering up kindling,
telling each other survival stories, the need for bodily warmth;
not daring to move closer in these singular times.

We all end up sometimes praying,
most more out of fear than faith, or desperation –
exasperation that all else has failed.

*Mick Jenkinson*


## Hibernation

With winter snarling at our ankles
we stocked up light, stoked the days to kindle
cold mornings into flame. Wore fur
like hair-shirts, huddled in deep caves,
moonlighting from this hibernation
for scraps of summer memories
to light the waning fire. And as snow
glazed the world to white, we snuggled down,
slept in a wrap of ice, not knowing
centuries would pass before it melted.

*Kathy Miles*

Transformation

In late November,
sodden leaves transform
pavements into brown rivers.

A black crow flies over
the rain slick road —
transmutes to a shadow in fog.

A toddler is crying — shrill,
ragged — it pierces the icy air,
turns all to frost.

*Elizabeth Kemball*




Winter Morning

The lingering moon
is a tilted cup.
It has spilled its milk
on the frozen grass.

The bleached blades snap
beneath my feet,
the iced veins split.
This too shall pass.

*Isobel Dixon*

First Frost

First frost of winter
Icicle thorns sharpen the scent

*Charlie Ulyatt*


Mistletoe

Suspended between the heavens and the earth,
Your fertile bough, which plants the kiss of love
upon the sky – the promise of new birth
Suspended between the heavens and the earth,
Tears of Frigga, treasure beyond worth,
The longest night, yet here begins the birth
of better days, of hope – you shine above
Suspended between the heavens and the earth,
Your fertile bough, which plants the kiss of love.

*Rebecca Lowe*


Ghost Apples

In an orchard of Jonagold trees
              encrusted with a thin layer of ice

autumn's leftover apples freeze —
              whose insides liquify, slip out of

their jeweled encasement, leave
              crystal shells behind — to haunt

in the first light of day, glisten
              in grey mist, and then melt away.

*Stephen Jackson*

## Murmuration

A carefree fluidity.
Beauty forming in chaos.
No leader or plan.
Just pleasure in flight.
Clouds of life above,
gathering in the dusk.
And as skies grow dark,
they rest in fellowship.
Dreaming of the long flight.

*Richard Waring*

## Dog in December

As the cappuccino of her winter coat grows in
The fur she no longer needs
Leaves her in a halo.
It clouds in small drifts,
A feathering,
A froth,
A seafoam
Churning up onto a bright beach
On a clear, cold
New Year's Day.

*Kate Dowling*

## Thaw

Pendulous in idle distance,
unwind windows and let out the miles,
wound tight like winter linen, put away
out of the prying light come spring.

Snap it back against the cobbles like a jump rope,
see if you can't take me back to that place,
un-nourished, soil as thin as glass,
to roof fire and the glisten of warm stone.
You are still stone, flint-hard and crackling.
Soften your palm. In opening, who loses?

*Alice Tarbuck*




## Old Town

Train your eyes up, out and along
this vista of lighted spires.
At furthest reach, the bloodied sun expires
and sputters out behind the castle mound.
You cannot reach there: everything is dips
and sudden bridges, plunging gardens, cobbled ridges,
oiled black North Sea muscle tenses, catches you
and throws you back.

*Alice Tarbuck*

## Snow Queen

Snow rushed to welcome you -
your brothers, each greeted in their turn
by storm and sun,
snowballed while you curled
into my body, not ready yet to leave
familiar warmth.
I held you to the window, showed you
the snow queen's dance and the whirling
of her diamond cloak, and hoped
no shattered mirror would ever blind you.

*Karen Ankers*


## Winter Sunlight

It comes low, striking houses, fence posts,
telegraph poles, stone dykes into light -
for miles, the land lifts an inch above itself
as grass and fern bristle in the sideways glance
of a great eye opening. Inky underselves
seep from gullies and hillocks struck visible.
And you: your breath, clouding
the hair of frost on twigs and branches,
the aura gleaming along a roof ridge.

*Jon Miller*

## Geese on a Field at Sunset

Breaking the pastel of the sky,
A plump clumsiness of form
Shaping a perfect Vee;

A tick against the ledger of the day,
Air horn-echoing with childish delight
As you come to land on a frowning glide.

In unsuitable footwear you gather,
Boats bobbing on a sea, unpicking
The woollen weave of the stubbled field.

*Ben Showers*

## Watendlath Tarn

No moon-fed ebb and flow
but lapping waves
lift rafts of winter reed.
Tide-less mountain water
licks at overhanging branches.
Distant somethings surface,
pierce black ripples, disappear.

*Kathy Gee*

## Winternight

Snowflakes fat as goose-feathers
falling quiet as murder

*Chris Allen*

## The Sun Seen from Winter Hill at New Year

Beyond frozen fog
white sun kindles scudding cloud
sets the sky ablaze

*Chris Allen*

## As Before and Before

Overhead, a heron.
Along the quay, a seal.
A tame air, still,
Winter in it.
The turning near,
And the measured
Lengthening of the
Light, as before
And before.

*Bob Brussack*

## Nocturne

For six months, we embrace
each other in darkness. Sun
shuns our wizened bodies.
We few, whittled like sticks
in careless hands, speak only
in whispers, in reverence
of that forgotten warmth,
as below our feet, under tarmac,
millions of seeds lie in wait
ready to erupt at first light.

*David Ralph Lewis*


## Nordmann Fir

I've strung her not with brilliant white
but kinder yellow lights this year.
She's meant to be a no-drop tree—
still her needles fall. I fancy it's
the heat of the bulbs, the years'
accumulated ornaments, paucity
of water that desiccate her fronds.
But no, for shame, the tree was cut,
ungrounded,
dying all along.

*Katie Jenkins*

## Service of Blue Christmas

Votives flicker,
stained etchings of the Savior
in lowered light,
rain blankets the roof;
there is room for my pain.

*Cindy Bousquet Harris*


## Frost Warning

Rain might reminisce
in ice,
black linens on an unmade bed,
winter's knife
begins to carve
on windows as we sleep,
on houses as we dream of rain
gone quiet,
glistening in the street; go slow,
there may be ice.

*Cindy Bousquet Harris*

## Christmas Angel

Next-door's angel has gone up again,
her spread wings flapping silently
all night. I wake and see her,
keeping her vigil - as if love, not light
flowed through her veins.
How brave she is, out in the cold and dark,
bearing witness to our midnight hopes.

*Sarah Connor*

## Winter

Everything cuts in winter -
wind, rain, hail - everything.
Winter comes equipped
with knives, all shapes, all sizes -
the gull's wing a smooth scimitar,
the hedge bristling with stilettoes,
even the robin's song -
so sweet
so sharp.

*Sarah Connor*

Fresh Start

Yesterday's swamp track
is iron-hard today.
My boots crunch and slide
as snow cleans my soles
clear of claggy residues.

*Ceinwen E. Cariad Haydon*


Sentient Companionship

When full moons light up fresh snow,
I dream of yetis. I'm sure I met them
way-back, as a child. Once, I imagined
friendship might be possible,
if I stayed quite still.
I walk in circles:
lockdown's diktats rule
*stay local* and *don't mingle.* Alone
in our nature reserve I see a shape,
maybe a friend, lumber through the trees.

*Ceinwen E. Cariad Haydon*

<u>Halcyon Days</u>

Daughter and fisher of kings, heartbroken,
drowned in sorrows; yet gods can show pity
too, even if it is in their own way.

Now you lay your babies on a beach,
watch winter eat the sun until it's reborn,
and you have peace, once every year.

So short a time, that. Though it spans eternity.

*Maxine Rose Munro*


<u>Up Helly Aa</u>

In the time of the darkening, wan sun
too feeble to climb beyond the horizon,

we light our fires and ice winds bite
at our hands and faces,

but still we laugh, speak in whispers,
for we are here to witness a change

and sing defiance of the black night,
burn it up, dance in its ashes,

because here is Thule, here is how
we give back strength to our sun.

*Maxine Rose Munro*

## Moonstones

Set in windows, at hand's reach,
milk-colored stones catch fire and hold white light

spilled from the winter sun hard-set on its way
toward snow-bright western hills rising, as if from sleep,
free of the havoc of our days gone wrong.

How did we find ourselves here, drawing mean heat from a star,
our days run out in rounds
like river stones washed through flashing currents

in dreams we visit nights to talk our troubles out to sea, where rivers end
unbound, eager for release to the moon's cold drawing touch?

*Anthony Paticchio*

## Feather

Walking the wind with ghosts and birds,
I find a feather,
Curled and intricate,
Beautifully camouflaged
Against bone-bleached heather.
I hold it up to show you.
You pinch it between your fingers
And take it with you when you go,
Spinning away northwards,
To settle on a distant skein of snow.

*Larissa Reid*

## Winter Soup

Making borscht while the snow hits,
makes me think I'm a bit-player
in a Russian novel; the fat cook
or the mother who has to eke the last
of the beets to feed her hungry girls.

But I set the table for two only,
blue bowls from Crail, the wedding spoons.
I catch the solstice in my hands,
pass it to you. There will be light again
and snow falling gently on us both.

*Lynn Valentine*


## New Year Walks

Iced footsteps left from yesterday,
the ghost of myself found again,
winter shadow hardening
in snow. Will I always wander
the same track? Listen
for the echoing beat of your heart?
On this path you walked, years before.

*Lynn Valentine*


## At the Wood Stove: One Hundred Seconds to Midnight

I turn this log as the year turns; smoke-darkened
hardwood crumbles to ash; red underbelly
glowers; an ember cracks, not yet dead.

*Jude Marr*

Evergreen

A tree can show me how to stand. Tall,
it will help support the sky.

But cut down when the roots are strong,
a tree begins to sag, grows weak, locked

inside a house when full of life. Discarded
much too soon, the body in the road

will stop me for a while to change my path.
A tree can show me how to fall.

*Jenny Mitchell*



Adoration of the Plants

It has grown. In this last year,
their breath shines green,
exhales towards the floor.

Inspiration climbs the air,
leaves curled across my ceiling,
reflecting the sparse light

edging through harsh clouds
to grace my flat. A field of pots
help me to cross another year.

*Jenny Mitchell*

19

Souvenirs

A pink Christmas tree the color of a kind of happiness
only children understand, and a church music box,
its plastic steeple surrounded by glitter for snow,
and ribbon candy curled like hyacinth buds,
and me – the only child there.

I wish I could find that room again –
walk back into it, greeted
with the smell of boiled chestnuts
peeled by my grandfather's penknife,
greeted with too many kisses.

*Colette Tennant*


Christmas on the Farm in the Dust

After four parched years of dismal rainfall
the bore was their only prospect,
since it had choked with treacherous sludge
there was no way to grow essential feed
fodder reserves were almost exhausted.

Regardless of their perilous circumstance
they were resolute that their young children
would still have presents under the cherished fading tree
lunch of roast meats and vegetables with flambé fruit pudding,
even in the blistering summer heat.

*Rob Mckinnon*

Christmas Visitors

On quiet December nights, when ice creaks
in nightcap glasses, the missed and absent gather –
swirl an inch above the floorboards,
swathe the deepest layers of the tree,
hover in the waver of low fire embers.

Evading form and shadow, they trick
fairy lights, dodge candle flicker,
seep away through air bricks
and up the chimney breast –
leave the loved and present sleeping.

*Eilín de Paor*


Cuairteoirí Nollag

Ar oícheanta chiúin, le díoscadh an oighir
i ngloiní deabhaid oíche, bailíonn siad atá ar iarraidh
agus in easnamh – scaobann said orlach ós cionn an urláir,
clúdaíonn said géaga is doimhne an chrainn,
ag foluain i nguagadh na ngríostine ísle.

Ag seachain cruth nó scáth, cleasaíonn said
soilse sí, ag lúbadh ó léimneach coinnle,
éalaíonn said saor trí aerbhrící
agus suas an aon tine – ag fágáil
na geanáin lonnaithe ina gcodladh.

*Eilín de Paor*

## The Wanderer

How long their stride, these stellar giants,
these wanderers reunited after centuries!

We raise our children and grandchildren
in padded wool-clad arms, breathing ice.

In another half-century, they'll point out
the same pairing to their grandchildren.

Hold skinny legs that kick the night sky,
gaze up, thinking of us, of this midnight.

Tonight, they are ours and we are theirs:
a pilgrim family, adrift in an unfamiliar space.

*Lucy Heuschen*

The "Christmas Star": a conjunction of Jupiter and Saturn that appeared in late December 2020.
It had not been seen since 1226 and will not be again until 2080.


## Christmas Eve

Mouths brandy-sweet with mince pie crumbs
we walk downhill from dusk to dark,
the gravel sharp beneath bare feet.

Lilting frog-rhythms greet our approach
to the dam. Between the willow shadows,
lights glimmer and weave.

Christmas fairies. They fly around us,
easy to catch; tiny life
pulsing light in our cupped hands.

We release them gently to the moonless night.

*Marian Christie*

## West Cork Prairie Rose

A slow extracted blink
and summer was spent.
Sap drained, skin wrinkled.
Carbuncular and crimson-hued
you shrank as veins bristled,
foliole turned inward.
We sought beauty in your demise;
in the fallow and the fraught.
The flood of pigment stemmed,
mired in winter's tight embrace.

*Lucy Holme*


## It is a Winter's Strain

This idle empty chill.
Green shed laddered by molten ivy
under the mardy sky's disdainful eye.

A column of wisped grey strokes the dusk,
bids the day farewell. Whispers
*Come; breathe night's fetid depths with me.*

Lichen curls, the waist-span of a moth—
circling in dark, unfettered whimsy.
Spins with the December winds.

*Lucy Holme Roberts*

23

## LA

He accepts the bourbon's
Fiery kiss
Now leans back
To let its warm hand
Soothe a silent apology.

Wordlessly I leave
Him to the only lover
That stirred his heart
The only lover
Not to walk away.

*Philip Berry*

## Snow Falls

Snow falls in the desert, a reverse globe
whose setting doesn't match the scene,
where rough bladed agave soften
and mesquite branches bow
beneath their crystalline capes.

In the swollen silence, ice startles & plunges
in frozen cascades. The saguaro
sheath their spines, stunned
by this chill bounty.

*Ingrid L. Taylor*

## The Warmth of Snow

Cobwebs of crystal thread and
crisp flattened leaves held the path
we dared that morning.
Coats crammed full spurning the
whip of air; boots sketching the way.
Sun's glare was too harsh to warm,
but the thrill of snow could scrape
winter's stinging grasp.
We were catching snowflakes as giddy children.

*Julie Stevens*


## Winter by the Lake

In grey rippling water, deep memories
of ice-days, coated black, smoke and steam
billowing in lost skies.
Men, huddled, dropping into darkness,
raised, emerging, coughing green-black globules
that sat, defiant, on frozen ground.
Nature, stark and cruel, has taken back
a lost empire as fingers of trees claw
in gelid air. It has bided its time.

Patiently snaking into every crevice we made.

*Tim Fellows*

## Childermas

The screech of an owl, wolves' teeth in the wind,
skies winter dark, barbed with stars.

The baronial hall is swagged
with holly, wreathed with bay.

Viper tongues of fire and candle flame
flicker light in shadowed corners.

A voice pierces the gloom, sings of a birth,
the wrath of a king and infants slain.

The song flutes, then falls away.
Through the silence, sorrow throbs.

*Iris Anne Lewis*


## Evensong

What saint was it who said
that when we sing

our prayer repeats itself—
its substance resounds

in vowels that lengthen like shadows
in the throats of hermits

who at night could fill my abandoned
barn of a soul

with the empty space in their howling
Salve Reginas?

*Dan Rattelle*

## When I Build My Snowglobe

In my snowglobe, I will position Dad in his recliner.
We will gather in the den
with Daniel distributing gifts, Kelly criss-cross
on the floor by the fireplace, and the great-grand kids
running ribbons among the dogs, Rags the cat,
and a mess of wrapping paper. After the season,
all, but Dad, will resume their daily routines.
I will wrap him in glitter sprinkled tissue. Nestle
and gently store him among other family treasures.

*Carol Parris Krauss*


## Reflections from the Past

That Christmas holiday, London clutched us with damp, fog-fingers,
and ghost winds danced in the crooked alleyways and over ancient stones
where kings were crowned, and beheaded queens
spirit-walked in winter-bare mazes.

In the faded-dowager elegance of the hotel lobby,
my sister and I dropped tea-time crumbs on the flowered carpet,
leaving a fairy-trail beneath twinkling green boughs,

caught in mirrors and windows reflections, our images
glowed and ached like December days—

the memories of our last family vacation.

*Merril D. Smith*

## I Don't Tell Anyone I Do This But

I hold something back, every year,        after burial;
boxes returned to attic's dust, their sparkle now shadow.

I hold something back, from distance,        something so small,
a simple thing, like I held your scent, the caress of your palm
on my chest, your breath on my skin when you were my being.

I hold something back, every year,        an old ornament
to pull out from the jacket of January, to remind me
that we're circular; that snow falls but the sun melts.

I hold something back, every year,        after the burial,
something simple, to recall how we once hung holly with hope.

*Damien B. Donnelly*


## Some Dreams are Designed to Delude

I decorate this tree with ageing ornaments
designed to return me to a past perfection
that never performed. I draw snowflakes
to delight these pages yet never discerned
their detail in the palm of my own hand.

Some nights slip beyond all explanation;

empty stockings over sleepy heads, daring
checks behind closed eyes before morning
delivers delight. Some things are designed
to delude; I hold spray before chopped tree
& without a single cloud, snow falls indoors.

*Damien B. Donnelly*

This Is Also Winter

It's a birdless, slow-drip morning.
The sky at ten is a bruised knee.
Trees wear ivy like fingerless gloves, and
Horse-breath plumes, giant, around stuffed haynets.
Wet telegraph poles, wires sagging
Stitch up the sour defeated grass.
At four, the sky softens to
The nameless breast of a woodpigeon.

*Sef Churchill*


Winter Night

I draw a line across the frosty pane,
clasp the knuckle bones of a tree
to feel the budding fingers
whisper promises to keep the faith in sap and branch,

and in the teeth of the north wind blowing
beneath the plum tree place a gift
for the vixen goddess of the night,

listen for the trailing music of her call,
falling with the winter stars.

*Jane Dougherty*

## Winter Morning Ablutions

A clean yellow line dissects the pillowed sky,
kissing peach on the edges, it stretches,
absorbed in evergreen shadow
and highlighted grey slate.
A cold yellow.
A dull peach,
but cleansing, clear-eyed; a promise.
Back-lit boughs lift their limbs in supplication,

snow is coming.

*Jane Mackenzie*


## Solstice Twilight

Clag hugs bare hilltops;
Blatters fill with siling rain.

Sough of wind at our backs
as we push through.

Wimpled wings cast
shadowskein on water.

Thunderheads threaten..
Earth hunkers down -
Caught in winter's stiff embrace.

*Margaret Royall*

## Winter

The magicians all have vanished.
Drumming fades into the distant peaks

as cold consumes the tarn below.
Near its shore: bones and broken oaths, accumulated.

Sky rumbles and squalls into white
noise, clouding and swallowing questions.

She dwells beneath ice: a specimen of surrender.
No swords rise from the lake.

*Catherine Fletcher*


## Logans

This winter we are logan stones, tipping on the tor,
The thaw will find us tilted and gasping,
Scenting distant gorse blossom on the still-cold breeze,
While cuckoos lay the illusion in their passing,
That we will not fall.

*Mark Steven*


## Lutein

My son's tousled hair
echoes the lutein gold strands
of pollen-heavy
catkins in the hazel copse,
gleaming in winter sunlight.

*Toni Lötter*

31

Christmas Gift

It is a time of gathering,
of holding tight, wrapping up.
Of course, there is excess:

here, a tree casting needles
of many-coloured light
through frosted windows;

there, the slow chromatic fall
of Chopin's fourth prelude
from a shrouded sitting room.

On a night giving little away,
I wander, eyes wide,
absorbing the residue.

*Andy MacGregor*

5,000'

The air gasps,

leaves behind
snow's essence;
iridescence.

It dresses the wind,
breathless.

*M.S. Evans*

## Advent Calendar

*in memory of my father*

Its wooden chambers, dovetailed joints,
miniature brass pulls, my father's design,
each small alcove sanded, each door painted
with images such as bells and angels, all
to point us toward a star, counting days

and bedtimes, when our boys opened just one,
brought to light a handsewn ornament of felt
or snowflake crocheted in fragile yarn
to bedeck the smallest tree, filaments of love
shining in the sequins, the sequencing of time.

*Elinor Ann Walker*


## At the Edge Of The Woods

Day seeps into December's morning sky,
pine-hung dewdrops turn to fairy lights.

Holly, strung with bright berry baubles,
punctures a dun sky pregnant with snow.

In dawn-soft focus, a deer cups her ears.
Doe-eyes hesitate on mine before,

silent but for a rustle, she disappears
under cover of tall trees and falling rain.

*Mary Earnshaw*

Christmas

The smallest words mean the most     Joy     Hope     Love
These things
Not things
May you receive them all
        A star            of particular promise
        A light           that has sought and found you
        The child         of your heart
Arrived
Waiting beyond the door.

*Angela Graham*




Christmas Gift from Granny England

Bubble, I called the globe that rolled, leaking,
from the English parcel. Moth-hands, moth-heart, breathless
for the burst, to pop this rare once-only wish. It must summon real snow,
known only in stories. Surely a fall so soft and clean, cool feather-
touches settling soothe, to melt all sunburnt Christmas hurt.

You'd seen eighty pretty winters when she tracked you down,
wrote you've a grandkid you never knew about here
at the bottom of the earth. Just enough time left to post
one fragile example – this broken world. Shaken wildly, impossible
magic. A fierce storm of glitter, settling briefly lovely, north to south.

*Ankh Spice*

Christmas Bells

Ten thousand stony hearts are cracked
by winter's icy cold
and sounds like bells
ring out across the hills.
Exhausted eyes look round,
pale flickers in the dark.
Hope wanders by these ways
from time to time
in tattered rags.

*Ewan Smith*

Clychau Nadolig

Mae deg mil o galonnau caregog yn cael eu cracio
gan oerfel rhewllyd y Gaeaf
ac mae'n swnio fel clychau
yn ceinio ar draws y bryniau.
Llygaid blinedig yn edrych rownd,
neidiau gwan yn y tywyllwch.
Gobaith yn crwydro ar hyd y ffyrdd hyn
o bryd i'w gilydd
mewn carpiau racsiog.

*Ewan Smith*

## January

On Boa Island, I startle a murder of crows.
They scatter into the trees. An injured pigeon,

still upright, turns its head. Its once-eyes
tear with blood. I leave it be, know

that it's too late, know that they will return.
Continue to the old cemetery,

to find the Janus figure I have travelled
to see. A two-faced head, tear-shaped.

One face looks East. The other West.
On the laneway back, only feathers.

*Billy Fenton*


## The January Tree

She is counting the folds in her skin,
'I'll give up chocolate,' she says, breathing in.

I am staring through cold glass at the January tree,
its bare wintry limbs drawn across the sky.

Perfect silhouette, a former self, lighter now,
allowing light to penetrate the room.

A new wind rattles, fracture lines open
across the glass, I see a last leaf dance.

*John Scarborough*

Wassailing Spirits

I idle under the apple tree - warped limbs,
damp smell of green, dormant blooms.

Eventually they come: spoon and saucepan clanks,
grins and ciders, bright toes cajole, blunt fingers creak,
sweet hearts enjoy the blush of dusk.

And they greet me. They sing & dance & racket around,
voices conjure bounty, enchant praise, nurture the new.

*Marcelle Newbold*

Wassailing

Day struck dead at sunset and night birthed
into a pool of darkness, lit by a cold opal moon.

Freya and her faeries tiptoe through trees, holding Solstice
candles at arm's length. A snowy owl swoops past,

mouse in talons; its feast contribution.
All forest folk gather at the hollow,

stack Yule logs, make fire, roll out a party picnic;
to feast, dance and sing. Across the ancient forest

two Kings fight through the night. At magic hour,
Holly concedes to Oak, it is time to make way for light.

*Gaynor Kane*

## New Year's Day

Spent fireworks on the road,
traces of powder, dirty ice that drains
and gurgles into grates. Greyness
hangs heavy, pressing on the snow-prints
of ghost cats on the lawn.

Droplets spit from the sky, we huddle
in winter clothes, lights dimmed,
reality and illusion blurred in an aching moment.

This day is just another day.

*Tim Fellows*


## Snow Comes

Snow comes like
a hunter, hidden.
It stalks the woods
on long legs.

A god of old, we greet it
in the ancient language; lichen
and stag.

An equalizer, snow
caresses trees, stone walls,

smooths
earth's scars with light.

*M.S. Evans*

Gathering for Calennig 2020*

Raindrops pearl the hawthorns
as dusk powders a promising sky
our holly's berries are already lost
we must gather our sticks wisely.

White and blackthorn never agree,
elder would weep and willow is
for the broken-hearted. Soft
sycamore is carved for love so
we choose her broken branches.

*Old Welsh New Year's tradition where an apple is decorated
 with evergreens and skewered on 3 sticks for collecting gifts and luck.

*Ness Owen*


Visitation (Mari Lwyd)

Horror a horse skull, bargain its bygone breath with death.
The shock and shake of shell flays the air with its ribbon trail;
flails, tails, natters, rattles against glass, thumps, clunks doors ajar,
stealing heat to slate-sheen street. It reels mocking here's eyes
and now's skin, twists out the old tongue. The mare's stare
stuns a mortal's grimace. It lays bare a man to his knees, scything.
He staggers, siding, sliding out from the hollow-white
skull tearing down. The crazed stars are its crown. The skull careers,
leers to fears, death's dance in time's town; draw it back into its sack.
Dumb it down to its dark. Another bargained breath exhaled.

*Matthew M. C. Smith*

40

'Winter Sunset'
*Inspired by the painting by Valérius de Saedeleer*

Pulled from canvas into silent curves,
setting sun peaches soft ripples over an obedient sea.

The tracks of day's activities will soon be
blanched into an unstained memory.

Bones of trees sucked black by winter's yawn stand deep
from the evergreens who hunch together in whispered conversation.

Cottages sleep at the foot of the mountain
whose top we will never see.

*Charlotte Oliver*

Osseous

Moonshine on mirror, it highlights me
Chalk-white, this face of bones,
My naked body of what is left behind after
Autumn's burnishing. Osseous, no midnight flesh
On this barometer-body of mine, ice and frost,
A season of reckoning inside.

*E. A. Moody*

Frost Picks the Bones

Frost picks the bones of winter
Where land heaves its dark lungs
Ghost horizon. Time as moving shadow

*Lauren Thomas*

## Winter Training

Two minutes more the call as daylight falls
and in the distance a bruised sky gathers.

Sixty strokes then the hail is upon us, forcing heads
to the oars' heel, our hands set like stone anvils

fit to crack from hammered cold, necks
shrunk between shoulders, legs become bergs

the hull full of ice - whilst on the water
the sky's white notes pluck the sea's taut skin.

*Julian Brasington*


## Darkness/ Light

We chased the light as we travelled, not far
but to unknown spaces cloaked in peace,
crisp fronds of frosted edges bright
with the silence only a lack of humans brings.

We stopped and played, refuelling on sharp air
which cleared a path through briared minds.

Our fires brought light so searing, we had to shield
the flames to see the blanket laid above,
flecked through with embers of ancient worlds.

*Giovanna MacKenna*

# Little Crosses

## I

And we wend our way home, my mother and I, leaving a trail of jingling expectations flashing on and off, on and off in our wake, uncontainable simulations of joy in every colour. And we say that was a good day wasn't it and we nod and move on and I carry the bags of a little this, a little that and a something extra special for someone, who knows who, just in case we are caught short and we never are, never will, not while her dear heart is beating still.

And on our way we come to the birth, deaths and marriages church on the hill. The one we won't be going to any day soon and don't expect to again unless, unless and we ward off the inevitable with a slick-slick brush-brush flick-flick on-off and well, simulations or joy, or both.

I forge on along the beaten track but she stops for a moment, looks up to the bell tower holding a wraith of a cloud passing the moon, slipping through from arc to arc, angel sky tolling silent night and she listens, spell bound and I wait. Then, she gathers her steps, shuffles on, catches up and together again, one wise old woman and one fast becoming. Linking arms linked to bags full of delicacies, trinkets and charms.

And who knows the shape of soul - maybe the moon? A slipped disc of pearl shine with angels weightlessly falling gracefully, heavenly hosts into that icy chalice of holy, holy night. We glance back but keep on moving, two owls gliding through dark air hooting hollow hallelujahs, gloria in excelcis deos, in the chill. December breeze blows a choir of wraith clouds and winter freezes still.

Then home trumpets around the corner hark heralding two off-white faces spearing through the dark, bag-laden wearies swooping in low to roost. I turn the key that opens the door that cranks the machine that sets everything twirling to an old familiar tune and the music box house begins to spin with life as we breathe ourselves deep into all that contains us, and the flick-switch lights sparkle everywhere and even the darkest corners are lit.

(To be continued)

*Rhona Greene*

# First Snow

## I

A blackbird tucks its beak in the snow shovelling crystalized berries, and hops around searching for something to crack them open. But snow has softened the landscape. When yesterday we took the calm for granted, the wind came like a tidal wave to a message in the sand. Clouds shed feathers: a mythic bird in an arcane process of rebirth. A hooded stranger in the distance sunk to a pinpoint like an envelope disappearing into a letterbox; my neighbour's cat accosted the cat-flap until it finally gave way. From where we stood the curtains swayed beside our heavy breaths. If there were someone in charge of this snow globe, they wouldn't stop shaking it. Barred from tenuous safety, the spotted wind cartwheeled shop signs, loosened fences, draped the bridge to the city with a glass-beaded bedspread. Mischievous preening. Too much of what we wished for. That's what it came down to each year: desire and its demise.

(To be continued)

*Zaina Ghani*


## Snow Falls on Tycoch 1963

I wake from sleep, roused instantly by morning's gentle light. Its dusty rays push through the curtains, worn and grubby at their edges. Listen close and you may hear, faint as mouse whispers, breathing from the bottom bunk and single bed.

Gripping the bed-post, I kick out from the loosened sheets and swing, acrobatic as a circus boy, to the saw-dusted ground. I take a bow to the exhausted toys and discarded clothes. While close to the bed, curled up tight, my tangled bedspread sleeps soundly on.

My bedroom remains as quiet as broken drums, on this, a stranger of a new day.

Slowly I wend my way. Passing the night light, dead in its saucer of water, then on to the window, I pull open the cold curtains and wipe a broad arc on the glass with my pyjama sleeve. Outside nothing moves, no cars or people. Neither gardens nor roofs are in sight. Just snow, thick and white, about half a ruler deep. A magic kingdom unspoiled and pure as things always are in the beginning. Ecstasy surges through me, a rush like the smoke and coal spit of the Swansea to London Express. I shake my brothers, still in their dreams, loose from their beds. I am speaking in tongues.

My excitement renders me temporarily incoherent.

*Dai Fry*

## Southern Winter

Winter settled on the edge of land
Today, with its small gift of snow
That only fell in drifts of
Star-frost flurries, fleeting
Under night's retrieval of the dawn

By the time the light was cast,
A shifting in the dark to purple glow
A freezing rain had come again
And stepped with tiny pools
Of ice across the glittered lawn

*Lauren Thomas*


## Heat

On winter air dead-cold and still
    the wood-smoke curtain hangs,
curls beneath my eaves, my walls
    ice thin against the chill.

Though stoked and whistling hot with spruce
    the hearty stove awaits,
it will not fill your frame with heat
    until you venture close.

*John Baalke*


## January Is

January is an old woman,
the sharp of mountains, the words
of a hammer, white owl's voice of the dead.

*Rachel Deering*

Winter, the Protector

Year takes me to her heart's-depth to heal,
wears dormancy, the scent of guarded timeless grace.

Berry beads, my blood-filled hope
feel safe displayed around her neck.

'Nothing to see here' she warns away the world,
as quietly
I sleep.

*Sam Henley Smith*


Christmas is Over

Step across the threshold into the dusk,
eager to move, get out; in lockdown.
The sky shows apricot, with long, dark lines of
mauve-grey clouds.
Street lights start up, hazy and haloed.

Past the undertaker's, blinds open, a swivel chair
spun round, though no one's there.
The wreath, red and green, lies solitary
on the brown, carpeted floor. Not for mourning,
a last Christmas decoration.

*Janet Laugharne*

Vishu

*"Yesterday is but a dream, tomorrow is only a vision"- Kalidasa*

Vishu, the New Year begins in the soft early dawn,
a bleary-eyed wakening to the exciting day of sweets,
new silken clothes rustling, pujas and feasts on banana leaves.
Mother wakes her to open her eyes, guides her to the decorated altar
morning dazzled by the offerings of fruit, honey, sweets
to Lord Krishna, the lover of butter and maidens fair.
She's entranced by the picture of him playing the flute
and her childish heart hopes the New Year is full of fun.

*Note: Vishu is the name for New Year celebrations in Kerala.*

*Leela Soma*


Winter

Berry jewel, eye of my heart,
burnished in winter air;
the glisten of frost crowns a brittle rose
caught in the dying year.

*Elizabeth Barton*


January

The pheasant sits
in the ploughed field, a
note of music

*Sarah Connor*

## Midwinter

is a grey cave,
but like Persephone
I've nowhere else to be.

I press myself like flowers
into the pages of books
and bring the outside in –

a circus troupe of orchids,
a butterfly palm by my bed,
lashings of vitamin D.

*Lucy Dixcart*

## Winter Stag

Breath clouds into frigid mist.
Snap of frozen twig
Under finely-turned hooves.
Crown of antlers raised
You pause between beeches
Below tracery of boughs.
And sunrise spills silver
Through your silent church.
King of the winter woods.

*Polly Oliver*

## Frost

A massacre of feathers blears white
speared across the morning window.

*Ant Heald*

River Walk, December

You've been finding augurs again, friable there in the darkness:
A grey heron picking its way through the winter beeches' upper branches,
The carcass of a season pecked clean of flesh;
The river, deepened with last night's rain,
Drowns the woods with points of silver and the pull of moon-tides;
A skein of geese threads moments of light through the tilled sky.
All around you night is fraying,
A constellation of shades rises and beckons you into the currents.

*Julian Aiken*

Hanukkiah, 5781

January almond trees bring the first light,
like the shammash that brightens the eight
candles in succession. Then cyclamen,
crocus, iris, a succession of colorful flame.

In the end, nine candles burn in a final
red burst of bright anemones
filling vast fields of possibilities,
blooming against the blameless night.

*Michael Dickel*

49

## Winter's Grace

Silent arctic phenom -
her tacit pain - squeezing the blood
from my fingers; the coyote -
commences her sermon; a deer, perhaps,
will be sacrificed to the Wolf Moon.

Ruffed grouse - learns to stay silent - hunkers down -
amid the haunt - as do I: so important,
not to startle - on this, the coldest night
of the year; better to accept the pain -
the strife - quietly frozen, in grief, and fear.

*Elisabeth Horan*


## Cinquain – Holly Hill

Iced woods,
a brûlée lake,
my rump chilled to a bench
seated in wintry solitude.
Old limbs.

A stack
of sawn timber,
bright sores of culled branches.
Next year's wattle fences along
safe paths.

*Sue Spiers*

## Artist

Emma Bissonnet grew up in Norfolk, studied Art in Sheffield & Swansea, and gained a City & Guilds in Printmaking on Gower. She has worked in conservation & gardening across Wales. Her inspiration comes from a deep love of nature. Emma's prints feature Welsh landscapes, wildlife and folklore. etsy.com/uk/shop/EmmaBissonnetDesigns facebook.com/EmmaBissonnetDesigns instagram.com/emmabissonnetdesigns Twitter: @EmmaBissonnet pinterest.co.uk/emmabissonnetdesigns

## Poets

Matthew M. C. Smith is published in *The Bangor Literary Journal, Finished Creatures, The Lonely Press, Fly on the Wall, Broken Spine* and *Icefloe Press.* Twitter: @MatthewMCSmith  Insta: @smithmattpoet Also on FB.

Adrienne Stevenson is a Canadian living in Ottawa, Ontario. Her poetry has been published in *Constellate Literary Journal, Still Point Arts Quarterly, Bywords, Uproar, Quills, Scarlet Leaf Review* and *The Literary Nest.* Twitter @ajs4t

Mick Jenkinson's second poetry pamphlet, *When the Waters Rise,* was published by *Calder Valley Poetry* in November 2019.

Kathy Miles is a poet and short story writer from West Wales. Her latest collection, *Bone House,* was published by *Indigo Dreams* in October 2020.

Elizabeth Kemball's micro-chapbook *A letter from your sheets // if your sheets could speak.* was published with *Nightingale & Sparrow Press* in March 2020.

Isobel Dixon's fourth collection *Bearings* is published by Nine Arches, who will publish *The Landing* in 2022. www.isobeldixon.com Twitter: @isobeldixon Insta: @isobelmdixon

Charlie Ulyatt lives in Nottingham and dreams of living in Aegina, Greece. He has been published in *Haiku Quarterly, Iota, Algia, Sepia* and *Hummingbird* (US).

Rebecca Lowe's first poetry collection *Blood and Water* is published by *The Seventh Quarry* www.seventhquarrypress.com. A further collection *Our Father Eclipse* was published with *Culture Matters* in April 2021.

Stephen Jackson lives in the Pacific Northwest. He has poems in *The American Journal of Poetry, Hole in the Head Review, Impossible Archetype, The Inflectionist Review,* and *Stone of Madness Press.*

Richard Waring has lived in Belfast during 6 decades, 2 centuries, and 2 millennia. He's 45 years old and definitely not a vampire.  He's published in the 2020 *CAP Poetry Anthology, Poetry NIs FourXFour* and *Black Bough Poetry: Deep Time* vol. 2 .

Kate Dowling has written all her life.  She is the creator/editor of *The Failure Baler* literary zine.  Twitter: @WaveAtTheTrain  and @TheFailureBaler

Alice Tarbuck is a poet and academic, based in Edinburgh. She is a 2019 Scottish Book Trust New Writers Awardee for poetry.

Karen Ankers is a poet, playwright and novelist, who lives in Anglesey and is currently studying for a PhD in Creative Writing. Her poetry has appeared in various magazines and anthologies and she published her first collection in 2017.

Jon Miller lives in the Highlands and is widely published. He has also published a poetry pamphlet, *Still Lives* (*Sandstone Press*) and is currently working towards his next collection. Twitter: @jmjon6 FB: jon.miller.3785

Ben Showers is a fledgling poet who lives with his family in Kent. Much of his poetry is inspired by the North Downs that fills his field of vision. Twitter: @benshowers

Kathy Gee was shortlisted for the O'Bheal International Poetry Prize and, in *Checkout,* set in a corner shop, performing with crowd-readings. www.brainginger.co.uk

Christopher Allen has been writing poetry in earnest for 4 years or so and performs in local theatre, open mic poetry and even a TV advert for 'Get into Teaching'. Twitter: @mydigression

Bob Brussack lives in a cottage near the Celtic Sea in the south of Ireland. He was born in Manhattan and spent many decades in Athens, Georgia. He tweets a volley of rebukes aimed at the enormities of American politics.

David Ralph Lewis is a poet based in Bristol, UK who has two pamphlets out: *Our Voices in the Chaos* and *Refraction.* www.davidralphlewis.co.uk Twitter, Insta and FB: DavidRalphLewis

Katie Jenkins's poetry has been anthologised by the *Everyman's Library* and *Acid Bath Publishing.* She has poems in various online journals including *Twist in Time* and *8 Poems.* Twitter: @liljenko

Cindy Bousquet Harris is a poet, a family therapist, and the editor of *Spirit Fire Review.* Her poems are found in *Nostos, Unlost*

Journal, MacQueen's Quinterly, and several anthologies. She lives in California with her husband and their children. SpiritFireReview2@gmail.com

Sarah Connor is a retired psychiatrist, living in North Devon, surrounded by mud and apple trees. Her poetry has been published by *Black Bough Poetry* and *Irisi*, among others. fmmewritespoems.wordpress.com

Ceinwen E. Cariad Haydon lives in Newcastle upon Tyne and has been widely published. She believes everyone's voice counts. Twitter: @Ceinwenhaydon

Maxine Rose Munro is a Shetlander adrift on the outskirts of Glasgow. She is widely published and runs *First Steps in Poetry* which offers free feedback and advice to beginner poets. www.maxinerosemunro.com Twitter: @MaxineRoseMunro FB: maxinerosemunro

Anthony Paticchio is a retired attorney. He lives at the edge of a forest in a small rural town in northeast Connecticut.

Larissa Reid lives on Scotland's east coast. She's intrigued by visible and invisible boundary lines in landscapes and how people relate to them. Larissa is a founder member of the Edinburgh writing group, Twisted::Colon. Twitter: @Ammonites_Stars

Lynn Valentine is working towards her poetry collection which will be published by *Cinnamon Press* in 2022. She has a Scots language pamphlet out with *Hedgehog Press*. Lynn loves snow, mountains and dogs. She lives in the Scottish Highlands with a mountain for a neighbour. Twitter: @dizzylynn

Jude Marr (they/ them) is a Pushcart-nominated nonbinary poet who writes to survive. Jude's first full-length collection, *We Know Each Other By Our Wounds*, was published in 2020 by *Animal Heart Press* and they also have a chapbook, *Breakfast for the Birds*, from *Finishing Line Press* in 2017. Twitter: @JudeMarr1

Jenny Mitchell is winner of the Poetry Book Awards for her second collection *Map of a Plantation*. She has won the Ware, Folklore and Aryamati Prizes, and a Bread and Roses Award as well as several other competitions. A debut collection, *Her Lost Language*, was voted One of 44 Books of 2019 (*Poetry Wales*).

Colette Tennant has two poetry collections: *Commotion of Wings* (2010) and *Eden and After* (2015), as well as the commentary *Religion in the Handmaid's Tale: a Brief Guide* published by *Fortress Press* (September 2019).

Rob McKinnon lives in the Adelaide Hills, South Australia. His poetry has previously been published in *Re-Side Magazine, Nightingale & Sparrow Literary Magazine, Black Bough Poetry, Dissident Voice, Tuck Magazine* and *InDaily.*

Eilín de Paor lives in Dublin and works in health and social care. Selected for *The Stinging Fly Summer School 2019*, her poems have been published by *Vox Galvia, Ink Sweat and Tears, The Bangor Literary Journal* and *The Stony Thursday Book*. Twitter: @edepaor

Lucy Heuschen's work appears in *Reach, Green Ink, Beyond Words, Poetry & Covid* and *One Hand Clapping*. She runs *The Rainbow Poems* poetry community. Her pamphlet *We Wear The Crown* will be published by *Hedgehog Press* in 2022. Twitter: @Rainbow_Poems.

Marian Christie is originally from Zimbabwe and now lives in Kent. When not reading or writing poetry, she looks at the stars, puzzles over the laws of physics, listens to birdsong and crochets. She blogs at www.marianchristiepoetry.net Twitter: @marian_v_o

Lucy Holme is a poet from Kent in the UK who resides in Cork, Ireland. An ex-yachtie and trained sommelier, she is mother to three small kids and has words in *Porridge, Poethead, Ó Bhéal, La Piccioletta Barca, Burnt Breakfast* and poems forthcoming in *Opia Lit, Tether's End* and *Dreich*. Twitter: @lucy_holme

Philip Berry's poems have appeared in *Lucent Dreaming, Black Bough Poetry, Dream Noir, Poetry Birmingham* and *The Healing Muse*. He also writes short fiction. His work can be explored at www.philberrycreative.wordpress.com Twitter: @philaberry.

Ingrid L. Taylor's work has appeared in *Zooscape, Legs of Tumbleweed, Wings of Lace: An Anthology of Literature by Nevada Women, Gaia: Shadow and Breath*, Vol.3, and others. She holds an MFA from Pacific University and was an artist-in-residence at Playa. She is a veterinarian.

Julie Stevens writes poems sometimes reflecting the impact Multiple Sclerosis (MS) has on her life. Her winning Stickleback pamphlet *Balancing Act* was published by *Hedgehog Poetry Press* (June 2021) and her debut chapbook *Quicksand* by *Dreich* (Sept. 2020). Website: www.jumpingjulespoetry.com

Tim Fellows is a poet and writer from Chesterfield whose poetry is heavily influenced by his background in the Derbyshire coalfields - family, mining, politics, and that mix of industry and countryside that so many mining areas had. Twitter: @timrugby1

Iris Anne Lewis is a poet whose work is published in *Artemis, Ink, Sweat and Tears* and *The High Window*. In 2020 she won 1st prize in the Gloucestershire Poetry Society Competition and was featured in *Black Bough Poetry's* Silver Branch series. Twitter: @IrisAnneLewis

Dan Rattelle is a writer from Massachusetts. He is working toward an MFA at the University of St Andrews.

Carol Parris Krauss is a mother, teacher, and poet from the Tidewater region of Virginia. She was a 2018 Best New Poet by the *University of Virginia Press*. Her recent work can be found in *Black Bough, Mixed Mag, Twist in Time,* and *Pine Mountain Sand & Gravel.* www.carolparriskrausspoet.com/

Merril D. Smith lives in southern New Jersey. Her poetry and short fiction have been published recently in *Black Bough Poetry*, *Anti-Heroin Chic*, *Fevers of the Mind*, *Nightingale and Sparrow*, and *Twist in Time*. Twitter: @merril_mds Insta: mdsmithnj merrildsmith.com

Damien B. Donnelly is the host and producer of 'Eat the Storms', the poetry podcast, the author of two poetry collections; *Eat the Storms*, his debut pamphlet and a Stickleback micro collection, both published by *The Hedgehog Press*.

Sef Churchill won a national writing award at age 16 and promptly did nothing about it. She is featured in 2019's *VSS365 Anthology*, and is general editor of 2020's *Glimmer*. Her latest publication is a chapbook of microfictions, *Dread*.

Jane Dougherty lives and works in southwest France. Her poems and stories have appeared in various publications, and she published her debut chapbooks of poetry, *thicker than water* and *birds and other feathers*, in 2020.

Jane Mackenzie lives in central Scotland. Her poetry can be found in *Black Bough Poetry* and *Shared Stories, A Year in the Cairngorms Anthology*. She also writes for children and her poems can be found in *The Emma Press* anthology on insects.

Margaret Royall is a S/listee in several poetry prizes, winner *Hedgehog Press* collection competition. Two poetry collections & a memoir in Haibun form. Published online and in print, most recently: *The Blue Nib*, *Impspired*, *Sarasvati*. Twitter @RoyallMargaret margaretroyall.com

Toni Lötter is a mother, poet, beekeeper and landworker from East London. She documents life's small and domestic moments because at five-feet tall and mostly being stuck at home, she too is both small and domestic. Insta: @tonilotter tonilotter.net

Catherine Fletcher is a poet & playwright. Recent work has appeared in *The Hopper*, *Kissing Dynamite*, & the concert series Concept Lab. She lives in Virginia, USA. Find her work online at cafletcher.blogspot.com Twitter: @cafletcher2

Mark Steven grew up in a superstitious Cornish village and escaped by way of a degree in Religion & Philosophy, drugs, unemployment and voluntary work to Edinburgh. He's now a parent, has a job, runs and bikes in the hills and writes whenever he can. Twitter: @markfsteven

Andy MacGregor is an ecologist and philosopher from Glasgow. He finds his inspiration chiefly in nature, and writes a weird amount of poetry about insects. Twitter: @macgregor_andy.

M.S. Evans is a Pushcart nominated poet and visual artist living in Butte, Montana. Her work has appeared in *Fevers of the Mind Poetry*, *Ice Floe Press*, *Black Bough Poetry*, and *Anti-Heroin Chic*. Twitter: @SeaNettleInk Insta: @seanettleart

Elinor Ann Walker holds a Ph.D. in English from UNC-Chapel Hill and is an adjunct professor at University of Maryland Global Campus. She writes mostly on her screened porch, weather permitting. Twitter: @elinorann_poet

Mary Earnshaw has poetry in *Black Bough Poetry's* two *Deep Time* anthologies, *Dream Catcher*, *Broken Spine* and *Spell's* online Advent Calendar for 2020. Twitter @MaryEarnshaw

Angela Graham is a Welsh-speaking poet and writer from N. Ireland. Her short story collection is *A City Burning* with *Seren Books* Twitter: @AngelaGraham8 angelagraham.org

Ankh Spice is a sea-obsessed poet from Aotearoa, where winter and Christmas don't converge. His work has been nominated for a few Pushcarts/Best of the Net, and jointly won the Poetry Archive *WorldView2020* competition. Twitter: @SeaGoatScreams

Ewan Smith is a retired primary school teacher now living in blissful ignorance by the seaside in N. Wales. He writes romance and cosy crime stories, is learning to speak enthusiastic and inaccurate Welsh and enjoys avoiding the jellyfish while swimming in the Irish Sea.

Billy Fenton lives outside Waterford City. His work has been published in the *Irish Times*, *Poetry Ireland Review*, *Crannóg*, *Honest Ulsterman*, *Abridged*, *Galway Review* and others. He was chosen as a mentee for the Words Ireland National Mentoring Programme in 2019.

John Scarborough has been writing for ten years and is a member of the Louth Poetry Group. For John, poetry is about truth and beauty. He has retired early to write and has work published in small press anthologies and the regional press.

Marcelle Newbold's poems have been published by *Wild Pressed Books* and *Maytree Press*. A poetry editor for *Nightingale & Sparrow* and a member of *The Dipping Pool* writing group, she lives in Cardiff, Wales, where she trained as an architect.

Gaynor Kane is from Belfast. She is published by *Hedgehog Poetry Press* and her books include *Memory Forest*, *Penned In* (co-written with Karen Mooney) and *Venus in Pink Marble*, which was *Black Bough Poetry's* 'Book of the Month' in November 2020. Twitter @gaynorkane

Julian Brasington lives in N. Wales. His poems have appeared in *Stand*, *Channel*, *Ink Sweat & Tears*, *Dust*, *Envoi*, *Orbis*, and the newspaper *Morning Star*. His poem 'Morning' was published by *Black Bough Poetry* in the *Christmas and Winter edition* (Vol 1). Twitter: @littorallines julianbrasington.com

Ness Owen is from Ynys Mon. Her poems have been published in *Poetry Wales*, *Red Poets*, *Mslexia*, *Arachne Press*, *Mother's Milk Books* and

*Three Drops Press.* Her collection *'Mamiaith (Mother-tongue)* is published by *Arachne Press.*

Charlotte Oliver was the commissioned poet for BBC Radio York's *Make a Difference* campaign and has poems published or forthcoming for *Spelt, Poetry Pea Journal, Pandemic, Ice Floe Press, One Hand Clapping, Poetry & Covid* and Not4UCollective's *Poems from Home.* Twitter: @charlotteolivr www.charlotteoliver.com
Insta: charlotteoliverpoet

E. A. Moody is a Welsh writer, runner and paddleboarder. They are published in *Black Bough poetry, Apex Poetry* with work forthcoming in *Green Ink Press* and *Seventh Quarry Press.* Twitter: eamoody1

Lauren Thomas likes writing vivid poems that deal with themes of passing time, memory, voice and the natural world. Lauren won the #BBmicro poem contest in 2021. Insta: @thoughtsofmanythings and
Twitter: @laurenmywrites

Rhona Greene is a Dubliner mad about the arts, wild about nature and besotted with poetry reading and boosting poets on social media. She is thrilled to have this, her second publication with *Black Bough Poetry.* Twitter: @Rhona_Greene

Z. R. Ghani is a 'Best of the Net'-nominated poet from North London. Her poems have appeared in *Magma Poetry, Black Bough Poetry, The Willowherb Review, Square Wheel Press* and *The Adriatic.* Twitter: @zr_ghani    Insta: @z.r.ghani

Dai Fry, Swansea-born writer, published his collection *Under Photon Crowns: Selected Writings of Dai Fry.* It was published by *Black Bough Poetry* in 2021.

Giovanna MacKenna writes to ease conversations about the difficult things which fill all our lives, but are rarely spoken aloud. Find her recent words in *Written Tales, Wet Grain, Dreich, Visual Verse* and *Dear Damsels.* Twitter: @giovmacpoet

John Baalke holds an MFA from Seattle Pacific University, currently resides in the Peak District, and has poems published in *Cirque, Stoneboat, Hummingbird,* and other journals.

Rachel Deering lives in Bath with a cat. Debut collection is *Crown of Eggshell* published by *Cerasus Poetry.* Twitter: @DeeringRachel

Samantha Henley Smith has a special interest in Bibliotherapy. Passionate about the power of poetry, she has work published by, or forthcoming in *Ice Floe Press, Post Script, Hedgehog Poetry Press* and the 'Best of the Folklore' Prize. Twitter @Fictionprescri1

Janet Laugharne lives in Wales, UK. Her work has appeared in *Atrium, Sarasvati, Writers' Forum, Litro Online, Spelk, Reflex Fiction* and *Paragraph Planet.* She also co-writes with Jacqueline Harrett, under their pseudonym J.L. Harland. Insta: jlharlandauthor

Leela Soma is an Indo-Scot poet, with two collections of poetry and poems in several anthologies.
leelasoma.wordpress.com/ Twitter: Glasgowlee

Elizabeth Barton is an artist and published poet from Aotearoa, with work featured in *Vita Brevis, Pink Plastic House Press* and *Spillwords* A winner of the 2020 White Label Cinq competition, she has a forthcoming collection of poetry from *Hedgehog Poetry Press.* Twitter: @DestinyAngel25

Lucy Dixcart lives in Kent. Her poems have appeared in a number of journals and her debut pamphlet, *Faint,* was published in 2020 by *Wild Pressed Books.* Twitter: @lucydixcart

Polly Oliver has featured work in publications by *Black Bough Poetry, The Wombwell Rainbow, The Tide Rises, Falls* and *Spillwords.* She is Pushcart prize nominated and was Poet of the Month and runner up for Publication of the Year on Spillwords.

Ant Heald hails from Yorkshire and lives in Llanelli, which influenced his contribution to poemofthenorth.co.uk and subsequent poems shadowing that project that emerged on Instagram - @antheald. He was awarded the inaugural Nigel Jenkins Literary Award, 2021.

Julian Aiken's poetry is rooted in landscape, and much of his work has engaged with the emotional resonance of place. His poetry can be found in *Acumen, The French Literary Review, Obsessed with Pipework, Marble Poetry,* and *The Interpreter's House.* Twitter: @JulianAiken8

Michael Dickel, an American-Israeli poet, lives and writes in Jerusalem. *Nothing Remembers,* his most recent collection of poetry, won a Feathered Quill Award for Poetry. He edits *The BeZine* online quarterly of literature, arts, and activism TheBeZine.com  Twitter: @MYDekel469

Elisabeth Horan is the author of numerous poetry chapbooks and collections, and the Editor-In-Chief of *Animal Heart Press.* Elisabeth is passionate about discovering new voices and mentoring emerging poets. She is also a fierce advocate for those impacted by mental illness. Twitter: @ehoranpoet

Sue Spiers lives in Hampshire. She writes with various groups - OU Poets, T'Articulation, Winchester Muse and works with the Winchester Poetry Festival. Her work is widely published and she has two collections: *Jiggle Sac* and *Plague - A Season of Senryu.* Twitter: @spiropoetry

Printed in Great Britain
by Amazon